## DATE DUE

| | |
|---|---|
| JUN 2 4 2005 | |
| JAN 2 3 2006 | |
| JUL 2 5 2006 | |
| | |
| | |
| | |
| | |
| | |
| | |
| | |
| | |
| | |
| | |
| | |
| | |

# Germany
## the culture

Kathryn Lane

A Bobbie Kalman Book

The Lands, Peoples, and Cultures Series

 Crabtree Publishing Company
www.crabtreebooks.com

# The Lands, Peoples, and Cultures Series

## Created by Bobbie Kalman

**Coordinating editor**
Ellen Rodger

**Project editor**
Lisa Gurusinghe

**Production Coordinator**
Rosie Gowsell

**Project development, photo research, and design**
First Folio Resource Group, Inc.
Erinn Banting
Pauline Beggs
Tom Dart
Bruce Krever
Debbie Smith

**Editing**
Jessica Rudolph

**Separations and film**
Embassy Graphics

**Printer**
Worzalla Publishing Company

**Consultants**
Sandra Schier, The Goethe Institute; Sonja Schlegel,
Consulate General of Germany

**Photographs**
Antique Porcelain Company, London, UK/Bridgeman Art Library: p. 18 (left); Archiv/Photo Researchers: p. 23 (left), p. 24 (left); Archive Photos: p. 26 (bottom); Art Resource/Giraudon: p. 17 (top); Ettagale Blauer/Lauré Communications: p. 14 (bottom); Collection Kharbine-Tapabor/Bridgeman Art Library: p. 28 (right); Corbis: p. 5 (left); Corbis/AFP: p. 8 (left); Corbis/Archivo Iconografico: p. 24 (right); Corbis/Dave Bartruff: p. 23 (right); Corbis/Bettmann: p. 25 (top), p. 29 (left); Corbis/Owen Franken: p. 10 (both); Corbis/Franz-Marc Frei: p. 7 (right); Corbis/Bob Krist: p. 28 (left); Corbis/Reuters New Media Inc.: p. 12 (right), p. 17 (bottom); Corbis/Gregor Schmid: cover, p. 11, p. 15 (bottom); Corbis/Peter Turnley: p. 25 (bottom); Corbis/Underwood & Underwood: p. 4 (right); Corbis/Vanni Archive: p. 19 (left), p. 21 (right); Corbis/David H. Wells: p. 7 (left); Corbis/Adam Wolfitt: p. 13 (left), p. 22; Giraudon/© Estate of Hannah Hoech/VG BILD-KUNST (Bonn)/SODRAC (Montreal) 2000, Art Resource: p. 5 (right), p. 17 (top); Beryl Goldberg: p. 14 (top); Sylvain Grandadam/Photo Researchers: p. 13 (right); Haags Gemeentemuseum, Netherlands/Bridgeman Art Library: p. 29 (right); Harris Museum and Art Library, Preston, Lancashire, UK/Bridgeman Art Library: p. 16 (left); Miwako Ikeda/International Stock: p. 12 (left); Jason Lauré: title page, p. 15 (top); David Lees/Archive Photos: p. 6 (right); Erich Lessing/Art Resource: p. 17 (bottom), p. 27; Rafael Macia/Photo Researchers: p. 21 (left); © Estate of Kaethe Kollwitz/VG BILD-KUNST (Bonn)/SODRAC (Montreal) 2000 Nationalgalerie, Berlin, Germany/Bildarchiv Steffens/Bridgeman Art Library: p. 16 (right); David Peevers: p. 3, p. 6 (left), p. 8 (right), p. 9, p. 19 (right), p. 20 (both); Kai Pfaffenbach/Reuters: p. 26 (top); Private Collection/Roger-Viollet, Paris/Bridgeman Art Library: p. 4 (left); Holger Stamme/Photo Researchers: p. 18 (right)

**Illustrations**
Dianne Eastman: icon
David Wysotski, Allure Illustrations: back cover
Kristi Frost: pp. 30–31

**Cover:** At a festival in Bavaria, a region in the south, a man wears a green felt hat decorated with a tuft of goat's hair.

**Title page:** A group of women dressed in colorful costumes participate in the *Oktoberfest* parade in Munich, a city in southern Germany.

**Icon:** A traditional hat, worn at many celebrations in Germany, appears at the head of each section.

**Back cover:** The *Heidschnucken*, a type of sheep found in parts of northern Germany, has long, straggly wool and curled horns.

**Note:** When using foreign terms, the author has followed the German style of capitalizing all nouns, regardless of where they appear in a sentence.

**Published by**
Crabtree Publishing Company

PMB 16A,
350 Fifth Avenue
Suite 3308
New York, NY
10118

612 Welland Avenue
St. Catharines
Ontario, Canada
L2M 5V6

73 Lime Walk
Headington
Oxford OX3 7AD
United Kingdom

Cataloging-in-Publication Data
Lane, Kathryn, 1969–
    Germany : the culture / Kathryn Lane.
        p. cm. -- (The lands, peoples, and cultures series)
    Includes index.
    ISBN 0-7787-9374-5 (RLB) -- ISBN 0-7787-9742-2 (pbk.)
    1. Germany--Civilization--Juvenile literature. 2.
Civilization--German influences--Juvenile literature.
[1. Germany--Civilization.] I. Title. II. Series.
DD61 .L32 2001
943--dc21
                                            00-069351
                                            LC

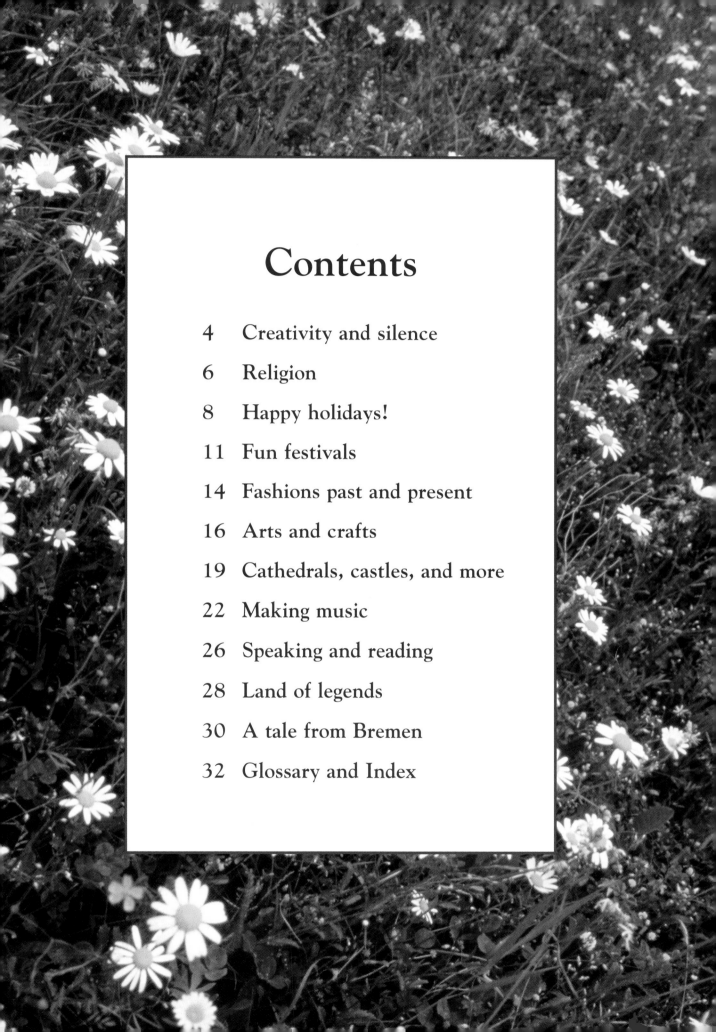

# Contents

Germany is a land of tradition. Holidays are celebrated with customs that have changed very little over hundreds of years. Folklore is kept alive through festivals and **re-enactments** of legendary events. Germans are proud of their rich cultural history, but they are also busy creating new forms of cultural expression today. German artists, **architects**, and theater directors, for example, are known for their daring modern work.

During Germany's history, there have been periods of great creativity, when artists and thinkers came up with new ideas and produced many important works. There have also been times when artists were discouraged from working, and people with new ideas were silenced.

## Artistic courts

During the 1700s and 1800s, the land that is now Germany was made up of different states. The land's many rulers wanted to show off their wealth and power. They built palaces and surrounded themselves with educated people and beautiful possessions. They paid artists to work for them as court musicians, painters, and writers. Many of the world's greatest **composers** and **philosophers** lived and worked in Germany during this time.

*Germans dance in the sand to jazz music at a 1920s beach party.*

## Berlin, city of artists

During the 1920s and 1930s, culture flourished in Berlin, the capital of Germany. Architects created new styles of buildings. Painters, and writers, actors, and jazz musicians flocked to the city. Berlin was famous for its cabarets, where dancers and singers entertained crowds. It was also the biggest film-producing city in Europe.

*Johann Sebastian Bach, a famous German composer, plays for the court of Frederick the Great of Prussia in this painting from the 1700s.*

# The Nazis

In 1933, Adolf Hitler, the leader of the political party, the National Socialist German Workers' Party, or Nazi Party, came to power. He banned modern art because it questioned accepted ideas about the world. Hitler only wanted people to see art that encouraged the Nazi way of thinking. The Nazis tried to silence artists and political **opponents** by putting them in prison and burning the books they wrote. Some artists tried to keep working, but did so in secret and with great fear. Other artists fled the country, including the writer Thomas Mann (1875–1955) and the playwright Bertolt Brecht (1898–1956), whose political plays were shut down by the Nazis.

Hitler spread hatred against people who followed the Jewish religion. Many Jews, including important scientists and **scholars**, left the country. Albert Einstein (1879–1955), a Jew, was one of the greatest scientists of all time. He fled Germany for the United States in 1933.

*Hannah Hoech was part of a group of artists called the "Dadaists," who worked in Berlin during the early 1900s. The "Dadaists" created non-traditional art which questioned society's values. Astronomy and Movement Dada is a collage by Hoech from 1922.*

*On May 11, 1933, the Nazis destroyed thousands of books in central Berlin at a* **Büchverbrennungen,** *or book burning.*

## East and West

In 1939, Hitler led Germany into World War II, a massive war that lasted for six years. After Germany lost the war, its enemies divided the country in two, the German Democratic Republic (East Germany) and the Federal Republic of Germany (West Germany). Some artists who left before the war, such as Bertolt Brecht, returned. Those who went to West Germany were encouraged to explore new ideas. In East Germany, artists were not as free to express their own ideas. Some artists were forced to leave the country, including the writer Günter Grass, who won the Nobel Prize for Literature in 1999.

In 1989, after 40 years of separation, the two Germanys were **reunited**. The new Germany encourages creativity and helps artists by paying for new work and supporting arts education.

Before 300 A.D., the people who lived in Germany were pagans. They believed in many gods, each of whom controlled a part of nature. Over time, the pagans converted, or changed their religion, to Christianity. Today, most people in Germany are still Christian, but there are also people who follow other religions, such as Judaism and Islam.

## The introduction of Christianity

Around 27 B.C., the Roman Empire, a powerful empire based in the area that is now Italy, began to **occupy** much of Europe. Three hundred years later, the Romans brought Christianity to the land that became Germany. Christians believe that there is one God and that Jesus Christ is his son. The New Testament of the bible, the Christian holy book, tells of his life and teachings.

Over the next few hundred years, the Romans were defeated. In spite of this defeat, the Roman Catholic Church, their **denomination** of Christianity, maintained its power.

*The altar of a church on Mainau Island, in southern Germany, is decorated with elaborate frescoes or wall paintings, which show scenes from the Bible.*

*Martin Luther made the Bible easier for common people to understand by translating it from the ancient Latin language to German.*

## The Reformation

Over the next 300 years, the Roman Catholic Church continued to gain power. Not all Christians agreed with everything the Church did. Martin Luther, a German **monk**, began to speak out against the Church's idea that people had to pay money in order to have their sins forgiven. He believed that God's blessing alone made them good. Luther was also angry that the leaders of the Church used the money that people gave them so they could live in luxury. Many people agreed with Luther. They founded a religious movement called the Reformation and created their own denomination of Christianity. It was called Protestantism because followers had protested against the Roman Catholic Church.

# Christianity today

Today, about 46 million Germans are Protestant and 35 million are Catholic. They share many of the same beliefs, but some of their traditions are different. Many German Christians do not celebrate their religion like their ancestors did. Over time, Germany has become more **secular**, but people still mark religious holidays, and celebrate weddings and baptisms in church. In East Germany, the **communist** government felt threatened by religion and discouraged it. Young Christians were denied a good education and good jobs. As a result, many Christians from the former East Germany no longer practice their religion.

# Judaism

The Jewish religion is about 4,000 years old. Jews believe in one God. Their most important teachings are written in their holy book, the *Torah*. Before World War II, over half a million Jews lived in Germany. During the war, the German army rounded up the Jewish population in every country it occupied and sent them to concentration camps. There, the Jews were either used as slave labor or were murdered, often thousands at a time. Six million Jews were killed in Europe during World War II. By the end of the war, only a few thousand remained in Germany.

Since the war, Germany's Jewish community has grown slowly. Today, it numbers 70,000. Most Jews in Germany have moved there from Russia and other Eastern European countries. They have settled mainly in the large cities of Berlin, Frankfurt, and Munich.

*Muslims built mosques, or places of worship, in the communities where they settled. This mosque is in Potsdam, a city in the east.*

# Islam

In the 1960s, many people from Turkey came to Germany in search of work. They brought their religion, Islam, with them. Since then, other Muslims, who are followers of Islam, have come from all over the world. Today, 2.6 million Muslims from 41 nations live in Germany.

Muslims believe in one God, called *Allah*. His teachings were spread by the **prophet** Muhammad during the 600s. They are written in the Muslim holy book, the *Qur'an*. Religious Muslims follow the main principles of Islam, called the Five Pillars. They must declare that *Allah* is the only god and that Muhammad is his prophet. Muslims must pray five times a day and give charity to those in need. During the holy month of *Ramadan*, they do not eat or drink from dawn to dusk. Those who are able must make the *hajj*, a journey to the holy city of Mecca, in Saudi Arabia, where Muhammad was born.

*Three Jewish children light candles for the Sabbath, the Jewish day of rest.*

Holidays are a time to spend with family and friends, eating a big meal and having a good time. In Germany, customs surrounding the Christian holidays have been passed down through many generations. People also celebrate Muslim and Jewish holidays, which have their own age-old traditions.

## Countdown to Christmas

Christmas, or *Weihnachten*, is the celebration of the birth of Jesus Christ. Although Christmas day is December 25, the Christmas season in Germany starts four Sundays before and ends twelve days after. Families keep track of the four weeks before Christmas, called Advent, by lighting candles. They place the candles in a special holiday candleholder made of evergreen branches twisted in a circle. They light one candle on the first Sunday, two on the next, and three the following Sunday. When all four candles are lit, Christmas is right around the corner!

## Saint Nikolaus

December 6, is Saint Nikolaus day. Saint Nikolaus was a bishop, in the Christian church, who died in 343 A.D. On the night before Saint Nikolaus Day children leave a boot by the fireplace. Dressed in a long red robe and a tall bishop's hat, Saint Nikolaus is believed to walk from house to house with a thick book that records how children behaved during the past year. At each house, he fills the boots of children who behaved well with candies and treats. Children who behaved badly get a boot full of twigs!

*(left) Children in Germany count down the four weeks before Christmas with an Advent calendar. The calendar has one door for each day. Behind each door, children find a picture or a piece of chocolate. A man peeks out of this Advent calendar from Leipzig, a city in the east. It is one of the largest Advent calendars in the world.*

*(top) Beautiful Christmas decorations and ornaments fill a stall at a market in Nuremburg.*

## Magical Christmas markets

Throughout December, many towns and cities hold special Christmas markets. The center of town is filled with vendors selling toys, candies, baked goods, and Christmas decorations. In the cool evenings, lanterns light the narrow walkways between stalls and the smells of hot spiced wine and fresh gingerbread fill the air. Nuremberg, in southeast Germany, has the oldest and most famous Christmas market. A young girl dressed as a golden angel stands high on a balcony while a choir sings below to announce the opening of this market.

*An enormous Christmas tree, covered with hundreds of lights, stands in the medieval city of Rothenburg, a city in the south.*

## Presents on Christmas Eve

December 24, Christmas Eve, is the day that Christian children look forward to the most in Germany. The popular tradition of decorating an evergreen tree at Christmas was started in Germany by Martin Luther. Families spend the evening singing carols and exchanging gifts. Some sit down to a huge meal of roast duck or goose. Others just have sausages and potato salad, then enjoy a big Christmas lunch the next day. On Christmas Day, families visit relatives, often staying until the next day.

## The Three Wise Men

On the Twelfth night which is January 6, children dress up as the Three Wise Men: Caspar, Melchior, and Balthazar. These men were kings who lived at the time of Jesus' birth. According to the New Testament, they followed a star in the sky that led them to the baby Jesus where they gave him gifts. In Germany, children carry a star on a stick and go from house to house in groups of three singing carols, collecting charity for the poor, and receiving candy. When leaving a house, the children write the year and the initials C+M+B for the three kings, over the doorway with chalk to protect the house against bad luck.

## *Karneval*

The festive season of *Karneval* officially begins at eleven minutes past eleven o'clock on the eleventh day of the eleventh month. The real celebrations do not take place until late February or March, when the streets of German cities fill with costumed parades and parties. *Karneval*, or *Fasching* as it is called in the south, is a time of merrymaking. People have as much fun as they can before Lent, a 40-day period when Christians, especially Catholics, express sorrow for their sins by giving up something they enjoy, such as rich food or staying out late. *Karneval* dates back to pre-Christian times, and was held originally as a festival to get rid of evil spirits.

## Raging Monday

The highlight of *Karneval* is the huge parade on *Rosenmontag*, Raging Monday. Spectators dressed in costumes are entertained by musicians, horses, and floats and try to catch candies thrown into the crowd. In the city of Cologne, the parade is a huge spectacle with thousands of musicians and hundreds of horses. It lasts for four hours, and ends with the *Karneval* prince, known in Cologne as "His Crazy Highness," riding on the last float.

## Easter

The most important Christian holiday is Easter. It marks the death and **resurrection** of Jesus Christ. Easter is also a celebration of spring and the new life that it brings. The day on which Christ died is called Good Friday or Quiet Friday in Germany. In Catholic churches, no bells ring on this sad day. Instead, people are called to church with wooden rattles. On Easter Sunday, Christians go to church to celebrate Christ's resurrection. Children search for chocolate eggs that they believe the Easter bunny has left in the garden. Real eggs are dyed bright colors, decorated with patterns, and hung from branches. An egg is a sign of new life. People also eat special Easter bread that is baked in the shape of a lamb, another symbol of new life.

*People dressed in elaborate costumes and masks take part in a parade during **Karneval** in Biberach, a town in western Germany.*

### The story of Saint Martin

Martin was a Roman soldier who lived from 316 to 397. One day, while preparing for battle, he came across a cold and hungry beggar. Martin felt sorry for this poor man, but he had no food or money to give him. He used his sword to cut his warm cloak in two and gave one half to the beggar. The next day, Martin left the army and devoted his life to Christianity. After he died, he was made a **saint**.

On November 11, children celebrate Saint Martin's Day with a parade in the evening. They march through the streets carrying lanterns and singing carols. In some towns, a man on horseback joins the parade and acts out the story of Saint Martin. Afterward, children drink hot chocolate and eat *Weckmanner*, sweet bread in the shape of a man. At the end of the evening, fireworks light up the sky.

*A man sells brightly painted Easter eggs to people near the Brandenburg Gate in Berlin.*

# Fun festivals

Throughout Germany, towns and cities hold festivals that recall their history and honor local legends. People have fun taking part in activities and dressing up in costumes like those worn long ago. Many of the best-known festivals take place in Bavaria, in the southeast.

## A frightening dragon

The town of Furth im Wald holds one of the largest folk festivals in Germany, *Drachenstich*, or "the stabbing of the dragon." For two weeks every August, people wear costumes, vendors sell sausages and beer, and hundreds of horses parade through the streets. The festival honors Saint George, a knight who is famous throughout Europe for bravely killing a dragon. His story is re-enacted with the help of an enormous, bright-green, mechanical dragon. Dressed in shining armor, George battles the frightening monster.

## A huge wedding

In 1475, when Bavaria was divided into many regions led by wealthy nobles, Duke Ludwig the Rich held a huge wedding in Landshut for his son, Georg, and Princess Jadwiga of Poland. The most important and fashionable people from all of Germany and Poland were invited. For a week after the ceremony, the townspeople of Landshut feasted on 40,000 chickens, 11,500 geese, 2,700 lambs, 700 pigs, 400 calves, and 300 oxen, all at the duke's expense.

The people of Landshut re-enact the wedding every four years, but without quite as much food. Dressed in **medieval** costumes, "guests" gather for a large party, with musicians and **jesters**. An elaborate wedding procession, or parade, moves through the streets, and knights on horseback **joust** in the couple's honor.

*After many close calls, George cuts off the dragon's head. Fake blood pours into the streets, splashing the squealing crowds.*

*Children parade through the streets of Dinkelsbühl during the Children's Festival.*

## The Children's Festival

For ten days in July, the Bavarian town of Dinkelsbühl celebrates the children who lived there during the 1600s. At that time, the Thirty Years' War, a series of battles between Catholics and Protestants, raged throughout the land. The Catholic town of Dinkelsbühl was completely surrounded by Protestant troops. Just as the Protestants were about to destroy Dinkelsbühl, a group of children, led by a girl named Lore, approached the army's commander. They kneeled before him and begged for mercy. The commander was deeply touched and ordered his army to leave the town. Both Lore and the Protestant commander are considered heroes in Dinkelsbühl.

Today, actors in Dinkelsbühl re-enact the meeting of Lore and the commander during the *Kinderzeche*, the Children's Festival. People in costumes from the 1600s parade through the town, perform traditional dances, and listen to brass bands play.

## The Oberammergau Passion Play

During the Thirty Years' War, food shortages made life very difficult for the people of Germany. They grew weak, and disease spread quickly. In the town of Oberammergau, in southern Germany, 83 people died of a plague that was sweeping across the land. Terrified that the plague would kill everyone in town, the villagers made a promise. They swore that if they were spared more deaths from the awful disease, they would perform a play, for the rest of time, about the last days of Jesus Christ. No one else died of this plague.

Today, the people of Oberammergau perform the Passion Play every ten years. The play is a huge production. It involves the entire village, with hundreds of people on stage at once. The play is performed more than 100 times through the summer and fall. Each performance lasts all day, with a two-hour intermission. Tickets are sold out years in advance!

*The most recent performances of the Passion Play took place during the summer and fall of the year 2000.*

# Oktoberfest

Germany's most popular festival, *Oktoberfest*, attracts seven million visitors to Munich each year from. Originally, the festival commemorated the marriage of the Bavarian Crown Prince in 1810. It has changed over time into a celebration of Germany's most loved drink — beer.

## The opening parade

Despite its name, *Oktoberfest* begins in late September. It lasts for two weeks, ending on the first Sunday of October. *Oktoberfest* begins on a Saturday morning with a parade. Beautifully groomed horses pull wagons piled with barrels of beer. Brass bands play and waitresses march onto the *Oktoberfest* grounds. The waitresses have an exhausting job serving thousands of beer drinkers in large, crowded beer halls. They carry as many as five *Mass*, or beer mugs, in each hand — altogether, about 55 pounds (25 kilograms) of beer and glass. So far, the record for holding mugs of beer in both hands is 21.

*During the opening parade of **Oktoberfest**, horses pull wagons with barrels of beer through the streets of Munich.*

*Although some beer tents have seating for 10,000 people, it can still be difficult to find a place to sit!*

## Tapping the first keg

Large beer tents cover the *Oktoberfest* grounds. At noon on the first day, the *Burgermeister*, or mayor, declares the beer tents open. A cannon is fired twelve times. Then, the *Burgermeister* **taps** the first keg of beer by hammering a spout into a wooden keg. The *Burgermeister* pours the first beer of the festival, and shouts, "*Ozapft is!*" which means "The keg has been tapped!" The beer tents can then open for business.

## Inside the tents

The tents are packed with tables and long wooden benches that each seat ten people. Roast chicken, sausages, and big, salty pretzels are sold in addition to beer. Apple juice and milkshakes are available for children. As brass bands play, people swing their *Mass* back and forth to the music, singing traditional songs. People also love to dance in the beer tents, especially on the tables!

 # Fashions past and present

German fashion designers are famous throughout the world. A few, such as Karl Lagerfeld, have started businesses that have turned into large, international companies. Most Germans dress as North Americans do, whether in jeans and T-shirts or in the latest styles for suits and dresses. At festivals and on special occasions, people still wear traditional costumes similar to what their ancestors wore hundreds of years ago.

## Flashy warriors

During the early 1500s, many wars were fought in Europe. After a battle, the surviving soldiers ripped apart tents and banners left behind by the enemy and mended their torn clothing with the bright, heavy cloth. Special soldiers from northern Germany called the *Landsknechte*, traveled around looking for work and adopted this style of clothing. They became known for their brightly colored outfits, with puffy sleeves.

*(right) Puff and slash became so popular that medieval royalty in countries all over Europe wore the style.*

*(top) Students in Berlin wear warm fall jackets made by German companies such as Adidas.*

The puffy sleeves of the *Landsknechte* began a style called "puff and slash." Sleeves were slashed, or cut, similar to tears in warriors' clothing. Different colored clothes underneath showed through the slash. Wealthier *Landsknechte* lined their clothes with brightly colored fabric. The lining was pulled through the slash, creating bright puffs of fabric all over the garment.

## Lederhosen

Among the most famous items of traditional German clothing are *Lederhosen*, which are Bavarian leather shorts with suspenders. Men wear *Lederhosen* at traditional festivals and sometimes for hiking. They also pull on tall wool socks and heavy black shoes. Sometimes, they wear calf socks. These special socks cover their upper calves and leave their ankles bare. They wear a finely tailored jacket and sometimes a vest and tie, with a white shirt. They usually top off their costume with a green cap that has a bird's feather or a fluffy ornament, often made of goat's hair, sticking out the side.

## The *Dirndl*

A *Dirndl* is a dress with a tight **bodice** and a very full, usually colorful, skirt. Women often wear an embroidered apron over the skirt and a puffy white blouse under the bodice. They may add all sorts of accessories to their costume, such as a shawl around their shoulders or a *Charivary*, a silver chain with hanging coins, attached to their bodice. They may also wear an embroidered white cap or a black felt hat. Bavarian women used to wear a *Dirndl* as part of their day-to-day clothing. Today, *Dirndls* are worn mostly for special occasions or festivals.

*The best* **Lederhosen** *are handmade using soft leather. A piece of leather runs between the two suspenders, across the chest. This piece is often embroidered with a pattern that is unique to the wearer's family.*

*A group of girls wear* **Dirndls** *at a festival in Bavaria.*

Throughout Germany's history, craftspeople have created beautiful pieces, such as dishes and bowls, for everyday use, while artists have used their talents to express their thoughts, feelings, and political opinions. Today, German arts and crafts are found in homes and museums all over the world.

## Dürer – Germany's master

One of Germany's most famous artists was Albrecht Dürer (1471–1528). He was known for painting beautiful portraits, but was also a skilled print maker. He etched, or scratched, designs into pieces of metal or blocks of wood. Then, he covered the etched metal or carved woodblock with ink and pressed it against paper to make many prints of a single picture. Prints made from etchings and woodcuts were much cheaper than original paintings. Dürer became famous in Europe as people bought more and more of his prints.

*Käthe Kollwitz's paintings, such as* **Scene from The Peasant Revolt,** *show the hardships faced by the poor and Kollwitz's hatred of war. In 1933, Kollwitz lost her job as an art teacher because of her political beliefs, which challenged Nazi ideas.*

## Käthe Kollwitz

Käthe Kollwitz (1867–1945) was a sculptor, but is best remembered for her political etchings and woodblock prints. Her style was known as German Expressionism. She used exaggerated images and hard lines to convey a strong feeling — often of the hardships faced by the poor. Unlike other Expressionist artists, she did not use strong colors. Grays and browns gave her prints a sense of sadness.

*Two people journey through a dark forest in* **The Flight into Egypt,** *a woodcut by Albrecht Dürer from the 1500s.*

*One of Franz Marc's most famous paintings is the* **Little Blue Horse,** *which he painted in 1912.*

# Franz Marc

Franz Marc (1880–1916) was part of the influential group of Expressionist painters called "Der Blaue Reiter," or The Blue Rider. The group was more concerned with color, line, and shape than the subjects of their paintings. Although Marc tended to paint animals, he was also interested in geometry.

# Joseph Beuys

Joseph Beuys (1921–1985) was an artist and a teacher who believed that everyone is creative, not just artists. He thought that art should play an important role in everyone's daily life. He created installations, or works of art that might include sound, writing, and drama, and were designed for a particular setting. He used a wide variety of materials in his pieces, including newspapers, hay, felt, earth, honey — even fat and blood!

*(below) Like Joseph Beuys, German artist Jens Gartelmann creates installation art. For an exhibit in Berlin called* **Temporary Gardens** *he covered lawn chairs in grass.*

*Meissen figurines in the shape of a saddle maker, a baker, a goat seller, and a coppersmith, decorated people's homes during the 1700s.*

## Fine porcelain

Porcelain is another name for fine china. It is made by firing, or heating, clay at very high temperatures. The town of Meissen, in eastern Germany, is a major producer of porcelain. Craftspeople there have hand-painted figurines and tableware for hundreds of years. It was the ruler, Augustus II, who helped make Meissen the home of German porcelain.

## Discovering the secret

Before the 1700s, only the Chinese knew how to make porcelain — that is how it got the name we use today, china. At that time, most Europeans ate off plates and bowls made of metal. The ruler Augustus II had seen porcelain that explorers brought from China. He was determined to start making his own porcelain. In 1701, he locked up a chemist, Johann Böttger, and ordered him to figure out how to make porcelain. Böttger was not allowed to leave until he succeeded. After twelve long years, Böttger finally figured out how to make the fine white china. Augustus II set up a very successful porcelain factory in Meissen. When Böttger, was finally released, he was weak and blind from the chemicals he used to make the porcelain.

## Cuckoo! Cuckoo!

Black Forest cuckoo clocks, or *Kuckucksuhr*, made in southwest Germany are famous throughout the world. The clocks are usually in the shape of a log cabin. A **pendulum** and two weights in the shape of pinecones that hang from chains help keep the clock ticking. A small wooden bird pops out of a window in the clock every hour to announce the time with the appropriate number of "cuckoos," the sound a cuckoo bird makes.

## Delicate work

Clockmakers must pay careful attention to the tiniest details. They have to adjust the delicate internal workings of the clocks, which are made up of carefully balanced weights and springs. Unique details and figurines are carved on each clock, such as dancing couples who twirl, wheels that spin, and chimney sweeps that pop out of chimneys.

*A clockmaker makes a final adjustment on a cuckoo clock.*

# Cathedrals, castles, and more

The dukes, lords, and knights of Germany's many regions built strong castles and grand palaces. Often, they hired the most talented architects of the day. Many of their homes and summer palaces are now open to the public as museums. Some of these have been carefully restored after being bombed during World War II.

## Cologne's cathedral

The delicate twin spires of Cologne's **cathedral** can be seen from all parts of the city. Construction on the enormous cathedral began in 1248. Bones that were thought to be the remains of the Three Wise Men had been brought to the city. These holy objects needed to be housed in a building worthy of them. The bones were stored in a three-leveled gold container, which can still be seen in the cathedral today. The cathedral is also filled with stained-glass windows, paintings, sculptures, and other artistic masterpieces.

*The cathedral at Worms is built in the Romanesque style, which was common from the 900s to the 1100s. Romanesque buildings are square and made of stone. Rounded arches, heavy columns, and narrow openings give a feeling of solidity and strength.*

*Construction on the cathedral in Cologne stopped after 300 years. The cathedral was finally finished in 1840, using the architect's original plans.*

## Castles of the Rhine River

Castles, originally built during the 1300s, line the steep slopes of the Rhine Gorge, a part of the Rhine River that is narrow and winding. Robber barons, who were powerful landowners and criminals, lived in these castles. They made great fortunes by stealing from passing ships. Until the 1800s, boats were forced to stop at an island fortress in the middle of the river and pay a toll to the robber barons. Today, people visit the castles while on cruises. Some of the castles lie in ruins while many others have been rebuilt.

*(above) Burg Eltz's many turrets, or peaked towers, poke above the treetops in the Mosel Valley.*

## Fighting for Burg Eltz

Deep in the Moselkern Forest, in western Germany, stands the enchanting castle of Burg Eltz. Inside the castle walls, three houses surround an open courtyard. The Eltz family has lived here since the 1200s. Burg Eltz is one of the few castles that were not destroyed during wartime, although its history has not been completely peaceful. The Eltz family had a disagreement with a local noble named, Balduin. He attacked the castle, and the Eltzes were under **siege** for two years. In that time, Balduin built his own castle right next door to help him attack Burg Eltz! Eventually, Balduin defeated the Eltzes. He allowed the Eltzes to continue living in the castle, but they did so under his power.

## An indestructible dome

Balthasar Neumann (1687–1753) built the Würzburg *Residenz*, or palace, for the powerful Schönborn family. The magnificent U-shaped palace has a sweeping staircase overlooking the entrance. High above the staircase, the world's largest **fresco** decorates a massive dome. Jealous architects claimed the dome was going to collapse under its own weight, but Neumann had made it out of pumice stone, which is very light. Although bombs destroyed both wings of the palace during World War II, Neumann's dome was not damaged.

*(below) The Würzburg* **Residenz** *has been carefully restored with gold leaf on the walls, a room of hand-painted mirrors, and many enormous chandeliers.*

*The Neuschwanstein Castle is ornately decorated. The outside is covered with windows, tall towers, and pointed spires. Inside, each room is filled with elaborate artwork and wood carvings. It took fourteen woodcarvers four years to carve the decorations in Ludwig's bedroom alone.*

## A fairy-tale castle

High in the misty Bavarian Alps sits a famous castle with turreted towers. Many people are familiar with King Ludwig II's Neuschwanstein Castle because it was used as the model for castles used in Disney films and amusement parks. Ludwig II was sometimes called the Fairy-tale King. He loved acting out German legends and seemed to live in his own fairy-tale world.

Construction on King Ludwig II's castle began in 1869. Rather than asking architects to design it, he worked with a team of theater designers who were more used to designing sets for plays than ornate palaces. Because of this, the castle is a fun mixture of architectural styles. The king died in 1886 and the castle was never completed. Today, tourists wait in long lines for a guided tour of the unfinished castle.

## The Bauhaus look

In 1919, the architect Walter Gropius (1883–1969) opened the Bauhaus school in Weimar, in central Germany. At this art and design school, students were encouraged to create objects that were useful, beautiful, and could be made in a factory. These objects were less expensive than those made by hand. The Bauhaus school has had a huge impact on design, including furniture making and architecture.

The Nazis felt threatened by the new ideas coming out of the Bauhaus school. In 1933, they forced the school to shut down. Gropius and many of the Bauhaus staff and students left Germany for the United States, where they set up schools and design businesses. The architects from Bauhaus continued to create sleek, geometric buildings that were built in Holland, Spain, Russia, and in cities across the United States.

*In 1965, Mies van der Rohe, a teacher at the Bauhaus school, designed the Neue Nationalgalerie, a gallery for modern German art. The clean lines of the building show the simplicity of the Bauhaus style.*

Germany has been home to many of the greatest musicians and classical composers of all time including Bach and Beethoven. The Berlin Philharmonic is considered one of the best orchestras in the world, and Deutsche Gramophon is a well-known classical music recording company. There is however, more to Germany than classical music. At traditional festivals, musicians play medieval instruments. Small brass bands, heavy metal groups, and popular dance music can be heard in Germany's many dance clubs.

## *Minnesang*

As early as the 1100s, wandering minstrels, or musicians, made their living entertaining in Germany's many courts. The minstrels sang a type of **ballad** called a *Minnesang*, or love song. They also began to write songs about religion and politics. By the 1300s, the writing of *Minnesang* had become a respected profession.

## Baroque music

Music of the Baroque period (1600–1750) is noted for passages with many quick notes and dramatic changes from fast to slow and loud to soft. During the 1600s, dukes hired musicians and composers to entertain their families and other nobles with Baroque music. Most Baroque musicians also wrote music for church services and played the organ while churchgoers sang. Baroque music was meant to make people feel closer to God. Georg Philipp Telemann, Georg Friedrich Handel, and Johann Sebastian Bach were major German Baroque composers.

*(top) At festivals throughout Germany, people dress in costumes, play traditional instruments, and sing the songs of minstrels.*

## Georg Philipp Telemann

Georg Philipp Telemann (1681–1767) was the most famous German Baroque composer. He wrote more pieces than Bach and Handel combined. He composed pieces for all types of instruments and wrote **operas** and other songs for choirs. He was always looking for new musical influences, so his style was very experimental.

## Georg Friedrich Handel

Georg Friedrich Handel (1685–1759) is best known for his choral work, or music written for choirs. He began his musical career in Hamburg, but later moved to England where he worked for members of the English nobility. He wrote many pieces for special occasions, such as the coronation of George II, King of England. Handel is best known for his English language **oratorios**. His oratorio *Messiah* is probably the most famous piece of Baroque music.

*Handel composed his first opera,* **Almira,** *in Germany when he was only nineteen years old.*

## Johann Sebastian Bach

Today, Johann Sebastian Bach (1685–1750) is considered one of the greatest composers of all time. During his lifetime, he was known more for his talent as an organist. His compositions were beautiful and intricate, but churchgoers complained that his playing was too difficult to sing to. Today, people around the world admire his pieces for piano and organ.

### The pipe organ

Pipe organs are enormous instruments that have to be specially constructed for the large churches and concert halls that house them. Many Baroque pieces were written for the pipe organ. The pipe organist sits in front of two levels of keyboards, with foot pedals below his or her feet. The long, vertical pipes of the organ may be right next to the organist or on the opposite wall of the building. When the organist presses the keys or the pedals, fans push air into the pipes. The air vibrates to create a sound. The sound can be mellow and soothing or loud and dramatic.

*Ludwig van Beethoven was a classical composer, but his music was different from other classical composers. His pieces were longer, more passionate, and required a larger orchestra.*

## Classical music

By 1750, tastes in music were changing and the Baroque style was becoming less popular. Composers started creating new musical forms such as symphonies. A symphony usually consists of four movements, or parts, played by an orchestra. Each movement is a variation of a tune according to a different mood and tempo, or speed.

## Ludwig van Beethoven

Ludwig van Beethoven (1770–1827) is one of the most famous classical composers. Born in Bonn, in western Germany, he studied piano in his hometown. He later moved to Vienna, where he was taught by the famous Austrian composer Joseph Haydn. He soon stopped his lessons because he considered Haydn too old-fashioned. Beethoven's music was very passionate. His pieces often shocked, but also delighted, his audience. He was said to be the most exciting piano player in Vienna, sometimes striking the keys so hard that he broke the piano strings!

## An emotional style

At the age of 30, Beethoven started to go deaf. He became depressed and locked himself away from people. He wondered how he would make a living and what would happen to his unfinished work. After months of worrying, Beethoven began to compose again. He was such a good composer that he first heard the music in his head and then wrote it down. His pieces became longer, more inventive, and full of emotion.

## The Romantics

During the 1800s, Romantic music came into style. Romantic composers thought of composing as a way of using sound to express an emotion, such as sadness, or an image, such as a beautiful landscape. Johannes Brahms (1833–1897) wrote dramatic pieces for piano and orchestra. These pieces also used elements of folk music.

*Richard Wagner (1813–1883) was the master of Romantic opera. His massive productions were about the many heroes in German legends. For these operas, he chose the story, composed the music, wrote the lyrics, and arranged how the performance appeared on stage.*

## Kurt Weill

Kurt Weill was a great composer of songs for the stage. During the 1920s, he worked with the playwright Bertolt Brecht in Berlin. Together, they created many popular musicals, including *The Threepenny Opera*, or *Dreigroschen Oper*. Many of Weill's plays angered the Nazis, who started riots during the performances. Theaters refused to produce his works, and Weill fled Germany. After some time in France, Weill headed to the United States. There, he achieved great success, writing songs for hit musicals such as *Cabaret*.

## Electronic music

During the 1960s, most German bands sang their own versions of popular American and British rock and roll songs. In the early 1970s, German rock bands began to create their own kind of music. Many of the rock musicians had studied classical music and were fans of the composer Karlheinz Stockhausen (1928– ). Stockhausen started distorting, or changing, the sounds of instruments using microphones and electronic machines. In 1971, he played a concert with the new group Kraftwerk. Kraftwerk later had a major effect on electronic and dance music all over the world.

*During the early 1970s, Kraftwerk was one of the first groups to use a drum machine instead of a live drummer. It gave their music a stiff, mechanical feel. They also created interesting rhythms by recording a sound, such as gears changing on a bicycle, and playing it over and over again.*

*At summer festivals and for special occasions, musicians play traditional songs on tubas, euphoniums, drums, and other instruments. Many of these songs are old favorites, and the musicians encourage people to sing along and clap.*

# Speaking and reading

*Two people look at books at the Frankfurt book fair.*

Germans like to read! One out of every ten books in the world is published in German. Every year in Frankfurt, a city in western Germany, publishers and authors from all over come to see the latest books at the world's largest book fair.

In addition to their love of literature, Germans are known for their skill at languages. German is the official language of Germany, but many other languages are heard in the streets. For example, people originally from Turkey often speak Turkish. Those from Romania speak Romanian. Many Germans also speak English, French, Spanish, and Italian, which they learn at school.

## German dialects

Today, most people speak a **dialect** called High German. While people from different parts of the country can understand each other using High German, the way they speak — such as the way they pronounce words or the dialect that slips into conversation — gives clues as to where they come from. Pure dialects can be hard for a German from another region to understand. For example, if a Bavarian from the south, a Mecklenburger from the northeast, and a Friesische from the northwest tried to have a conversation in their pure dialects, they would have a difficult time communicating!

## Celebrating Goethe

Many authors are celebrated in Germany, especially Johann Wolfgang von Goethe (1749–1832). Goethe wrote plays, novels, short stories, and poems. He was also a painter, musician, and politician. In 1999, Germans held parties for the 250th anniversary of his birth. All year, Goethe's birthplace, Frankfurt, held special events in his honor.

The Goethe Institute is Germany's national cultural center. It has offices in many large cities around the world. The Institute offers German language courses, organizes performances and lectures by Germans, and lends German books and videos.

| English | German |
|---|---|
| Hello | *Guten Tag* |
| How are you? | *Wie geht es Ihnen?* |
| I am very well. | *Mir geht's gut.* |
| Do you speak German? | *Sprechen sie Deutsch?* |
| Yes | *Ja* |
| No | *Nein* |
| Please | *Bitte* |
| Thank you very much | *Danke schön* |
| Good bye | *Auf Wiedersehen* |
| See ya! | *Tschüss!* |

## Speak a little German!

German and English are closely related. A few German words, such as *haus* and *glas*, might sound familiar: one means house, the other means glass. Even though some words are easy for an English speaker to understand, German is still a difficult language to learn because the grammar is very complicated.

## Scribes

Until the 1400s, most books were written by hand. Scribes, or book copiers, wrote carefully with quill pens, made from feathers, on sheets of vellum, made from animal skin. The work was extremely boring, so the scribes drew beautiful decorations around the text, making each book an original. Tired scribes sometimes missed an entire section of text, while creative scribes added passages of their own writing! No one knew if the words in books were always those of the author.

## Pricey books

Back then, very few people knew how to write, which led to a shortage of scribes. This shortage, and the months that it took each scribe to copy a book, meant that books were incredibly expensive. Only the very rich could afford them.

## Movable type

In 1455, Johannes Gutenberg, of Mainz, in western Germany, created one of the greatest inventions of all time — movable type. Movable type was a fast and efficient way of printing books. Gutenberg made thousands of tiny pieces of metal, each with a backwards letter on it. These pieces were set in a wooden frame to make a backwards image of a finished page. The metal pieces in the frame were then covered with ink. A piece of paper was pressed firmly against them, resulting in a page of printed text. Although the metal letters were reversed, or backwards, their imprint, or mark, on the paper could be read forwards.

## Making corrections

Using a press to make books was not new. Some books were printed from carved blocks of wood. This method required very skilled wood carvers who took a long time to produce a block. If someone found a mistake, the whole block had to be carved over again. Movable type meant that a person simply picked the letters and placed them in the frame. When there was a mistake, a few metal pieces could be moved and the page reprinted.

*Gutenberg's invention, the movable type machine, can still be seen in museums such as the Gutenberg Museum in Mainz.*

Dark forests with mysterious noises; castles with stone staircases winding through tall towers; knights in armor riding off to unknown lands. All these have inspired Germany's storytellers.

## Remembering the stories

Germany has a rich tradition of folklore. Originally, tales were passed on by word of mouth, from one generation to the next. When people realized that their stories may not be remembered, they started to write them down. Today, people can visit the forests, castles, and towns where many German tales take place. A scenic route, known as the Fairy Tale Route, runs from Bremen in the north to Frankfurt in the center of the country. Along this route, museums, monuments, and theaters celebrate the many writers, storytellers, and characters of Germany's stories.

*Baron Münchhausen has the ability to fly in this drawing from a book published in the early 1900s.*

## Baron Münchhausen

Karl Friedrich Hieronymous von Münchhausen lived during the 1700s in Bodenwerder, in central Germany. He traveled a great deal, but it is impossible to know exactly how much. According to Münchhausen's stories, he went to the moon twice, journeyed to the center of the earth, and sailed across a sea of milk to an island of cheese. He was almost eaten by a crocodile, a lion, and a bear. He saved a sinking ship by plugging the leak with his behind, and killed a wolf by reaching down its throat and turning it inside out. In Germany, people call him the *Lügenbaron*, the "Liar Baron," because he had a tendency to exaggerate. But in his hometown of Bodenwerder, people are proud of his imagination and they re-enact many of his adventures.

*A house in Oberammergau is painted with scenes from "Hansel and Gretel," a German fairy-tale.*

# The fearless Siegfried

Siegfried was a favorite hero in **myths** told by the ancient people of northeastern Europe. His story is told over and over again by the German people. The son of gods, Siegfried was a brave warrior who felt no fear. His life was filled with many adventures, including killing 700 soldiers in a single battle and slaying the awful dragon Fafner. Around the year 1200, an unknown writer wrote a long poem called the *Nibelungenlied*, "The song of the Nibelung." The *Nibelungenlied* brought together many legends about Siegfried. It told how he won the love of the princess Kriemhild, how Siegfried was killed, and how Kriemhild took revenge on his murderer. The composer Richard Wagner wrote a series of operas based on Siegfried's adventures. Together, these are called "The Ring of the Nibelung."

*Siegfried battles a terrible dragon, while Kriemhild hides her eyes, in this painting from the 1900s.*

*"Little Red Riding Hood" is one of the best-known stories by the Brothers Grimm.*

## The Brothers Grimm

During the 1800s, the scholars Jacob and Wilhelm Grimm began a major project. They traveled around the country recording the tales of storytellers. In 1857, they published a book of 200 folktales, including "Little Red Riding Hood," "Hansel and Gretel," and "Snow White and the Seven Dwarfs." Over time, the book was translated into many different languages, and German folktales became popular with children all over the world.

#  A tale from Bremen

Bremen is a town in northwest Germany. Many children know of this town because of the Grimm Brothers' fairy tale "The Bremen Town Musicians."

## The Bremen Town Musicians

A donkey who had carried heavy loads for his master his whole life was growing old. The master could see that his donkey was no longer of use to him, so he stopped feeding him. The donkey, realizing that his master was trying to starve him to death, set out on the road to Bremen. "There," he said, "I could surely work as a town musician."

After walking a little while, he came across a dog panting and wheezing by the roadside. The donkey asked him what the trouble was.

"I used to hunt with my master, but my speed is not what it used to be. My master thinks I would be better off dead. Now what am I to do?"

"I'm heading to Bremen to become a town musician. Why not join me?"

The dog gave a weak wag of his tail and joined his new friend on the road to Bremen. Soon, they came across an unhappy cat. The donkey asked her why she looked so sad.

"I have spent my life chasing mice for my mistress. My old bones ache and my teeth are no longer sharp. I'm ready to curl up beside a warm stove and spend the rest of my days purring. My mistress, however, would rather drown me than see me laying about. Now what am I to do?"

"Why not join us as Bremen town musicians?"

The cat liked this idea, so she joined them on their slow journey to Bremen. Soon, they came across a rooster crying at the top of his lungs. The donkey asked why he was wailing so much.

"Ooooohhhh, I am doomed!" sobbed the poor rooster. "After years of waking my mistress with my reliable crowing, she has decided to serve me tomorrow night for dinner. Now what am I to do?"

"Come along with us to work as musicians."

The rooster cheered up right away and joined the group. Soon they became tired and hungry. In the distance, the rooster spotted a faint light coming from a large farmhouse. When the Bremen town musicians reached the house, the donkey leaned his hooves against the open window and looked inside. "I see a band of robbers enjoying a wonderful feast," he said. "If only we could be in their place."

All the animals wanted to see, so the dog jumped onto the donkey's back, the cat leaped onto the dog, and the rooster perched on the cat. Suddenly, the donkey slipped and the Bremen town musicians fell in through the window. The terrible noise scared the robbers, who ran screaming from the house. Thrilled at their good luck, the four friends sat down at the table and finished the robbers' feast.

Soon, they were ready for bed. The donkey found a comfortable pile of hay in the yard, the dog curled up behind the door, the cat nestled beside the warm stove, and the rooster settled on the roof.

The robbers watched the house. When they saw the lights go out, one of them decided to go investigate. The robber opened the farmhouse door quietly and approached the stove to light a fire. Mistaking the cat's eyes for glowing coals, he put a lit match right up to the cat's face. The cat leaped up and scratched the robber's face. The robber stumbled back in pain, tripping over the dog who bit his leg. Then, the robber ran into the yard, where the donkey gave him a good kick. All this commotion woke the rooster who crowed "cock-a-doodle-doo!"

The robber ran back to his companions as fast as he could. When they asked him what happened, he said, "A terrible witch scratched me with her nails, then a man, waiting by the door, stabbed me with a knife. A horrible monster lying in the yard thumped me with a wooden club and a judge, who was sitting on the roof, yelled 'Cook the rascal in a stew!'"

The robbers dared not go back to the house ever again, and the Bremen town musicians liked it so much that they never left.

# Glossary

**architect** A person who designs buildings
**ballad** A song that tells a story
**bodice** A tight-fitting piece of clothing that is worn over a blouse like a vest
**cathedral** A large church
**Communist** A system of government in which the state controls the economy and private ownership is banned
**composer** A person who writes music
**denomination** A religious group within a faith
**dialect** A version of a language
**fresco** An image painted on wet plaster
**jester** A clown in medieval courts
**joust** A contest between two knights on horseback who fight with weapons called lances
**medieval** Belonging to the period of history from 500 A.D. to 1450 A.D., known as the Middle Ages
**monk** A member of a male religious community who has taken certain vows, such as silence and poverty
**myth** A legend or story that explains mysterious events or ideas
**occupy** To invade and control a country, as by a foreign army

**opera** A theathrical play set to music
**opponent** A person who acts against another person
**oratorio** A musical performance without costumes, scenery, or dramatic action, which tells a sacred story
**pendulum** An object that swings back and forth to keep a clock ticking
**philosopher** A person who studies the laws of the universe
**prophet** A person who is believed to speak on behalf of a god
**re-enactment** A play that recreates an historical event
**reunited** Joined together
**resurrection** The act of rising from the dead or coming back to life
**saint** A person through whom God has performed miracles, according to the Christian church
**secular** Not religious, worldly
**scholar** A very knowledgeable person
**siege** The act of surrounding of a city or fortress in order to capture it
**tap** To remove a plug

# Index

1 2 3 4 5 6 7 8 9 0  Printed in the USA  0 9 8 7 6 5 4 3 2 1